Portraits

Portraits

POEMS BY JULIANA HARRIS

Portraits, ©2018 Juliana Harris

All rights reserved. No part of this book may be reproduced or translated in any form or by any means, digital, electronic, or mechanical, including photocopying, recording, or by any information storage and retrieval system, without permission in writing from the publisher, except for the use of brief quotations in a book review or related article.

ISBN 978-0-692-12154-2

Printed in the U.S.A.

Contents

Self-Portrait	3
Family Secrets	4
The Mirror	5
My Sister Is Afraid	6
My Two Great-Uncles	8
Great Aunt Ellie	10
Great Aunt Margaret	12
Daddyfather	14
Great Uncle Dan	16
Family Portraits	18
Lillian Hellman, Eat Your Heart Out	19
A Hard Act to Follow (Marriage)	21
Backseat Driver	23
Shared Custody	24
Loss	25
Grandchildren	28
Reflections	29
Blake, Age Two	30
Pre-School Graduation	31
A Wish For Cinderella	32
Two Hands	33
Sex Ed 101	34
To Elizabeth Grace	35
Quinn Age Six (And A Half)	36
"I'm Glad"	37
Words	38

Family Secrets

Self-Portrait

Looking back at life
I see

The child
Who didn't belong

The daughter
Who lost her mother's love

The girl
Who dreaded mirrors

The actress
Who won awards

The wife
Who was blind

The mother
Who adored her children

The singer
Who found her song

The poet
Who wrote these lines

Family Secrets

My grandson Jacob
has a secret.
I wonder
what he whispers
to his father.

Something happened at school
my daughter tells me.
He wanted to tell you
but I said no
it would upset you.

I am hurt
until I remember
I never told my father
my first husband
tried to strangle me.

It would have upset him.

The Mirror

Don't kid yourself
my grandmother warned me
when I was 30
and she 84

I'm just like you inside
I look in the mirror
and think
Who's that old hag?

Now,
past midlife,
I look in my mirror
and hear her words

And
sometimes
I glimpse her face

My Sister Is Afraid
⊙

Afraid she is losing her mind
which is not surprising
considering the strain of madness
that pervades our family
like a dark stream
snaking its way
through an underground cavern.

Our grandmother
began her descent to despair
with blinding migraines
progressing into a darkness
which kept her immobilized.
When I asked her how she could endure shock therapy
she answered, "If you felt as I do,
you would do anything to make it stop."

Our aunt,
gifted by vengeful gods
with beauty and talent,
fought the same demon
in another way.
Her symptoms manifested
in maladies
which literally crippled her,
leaving her helpless on her own bed of pain.

And now it flows
to my sister,
who echoes the words
I remember from other lips.
"I can't cope."
"I'm afraid."
And I wonder
why I have been spared.

My Two Great-Uncles

❖

Uncle Dick,
generous and garrulous
(both to a fault),
wore high-topped black brogans
and drank only Old Overholt.
He delighted in
taking out his false teeth
to amuse me
when I was three.
A sepia photograph
shows him
at the wheel
of his Stutz Bearcat
which he drove cross country
in 1915
setting a world record.

Uncle John
lived under his brother-in-law's roof
as a non-paying guest
for forty years,
doted upon by his older sister,
as he was by most women.
Tall, handsome and charming
he would mutter "shut up"
at the dinner table.
as his host recited verbatim
an article he had read
in *The Saturday Evening Post*.
He never married
and died two years
before Uncle Dick who, of course,
presided at the post-funeral lunch.

Great Aunt Ellie
◉

Although she stood just a smidge under five feet,

she ran the farm like the Rock Island Line,

turning the crank to make peach ice cream I can taste to this day,

brewing dandelion wine that blew the doors off the cyclone cellar,

wringing the neck of a chicken as I watched in terror and awe.

She finished her day with a "boibun and branch"

spoken in the soft Kentucky drawl that would follow her

to her well-earned rest at age 91.

She left behind three heart-broken men:

The husband who saved her from spinsterhood,

marrying her when he was 33 and she 42;

the wastrel brother to whom

she gave room, board and adoration for 40 years

and my father, the child of a sister who couldn't cope,

whom she raised as the son her womb couldn't provide.

GREAT AUNT MARGARET
◉

Uncle John's fraternal twin
was his polar opposite
except for their
high cheekbones.

Unlike her brother, she married early.
Uncle Bob,
scion of a prosperous family
from Abilene.

Rumor has it
as Uncle Bob
lay dying of
cirrhosis

Aunt Margaret
came to visit
and he screamed
at the sight of her.

After his death
she got religion
and became
a Sufi

informing my grandmother
she couldn't be buried
in the black gown
with the cut steel beading

because wearing black
prevented the soul
from leaving
the body.

But "Dear"
got the best of her.
She donated her body
to science.

DADDYFATHER
◘

That's what I called him
because that's how we were introduced.
I called my grandmother "Dear"
because that's what her husband called her.

I remember
his hoarse voice
punctuated with barks of laughter
cigarette constant in his hand.

On his trips from Salina to Kansas City
he seldom passed the outstretched thumb
    of a serviceman,
arriving at our door with his Oldsmobile sedan
full of smiling young men in khaki clothes.

I, at age four, was enchanted to be the center
    of their attention.
I'm sure mother was less than pleased
to have these extra guests at her dinner table
although Daddyfather always brought along
    an extra steak...or three.

When I was eight his generous heart imploded.
All those cigarettes, I suppose.
The family doctor decided
"It would be good for the child to attend a funeral."

He lay, still at last, a pink-faced doll in a satin box.
At the cemetery I sat beside my sobbing grandmother.
The box stood at the top of a hill
and, when I turned to touch her hand,
    it was gone.

GREAT UNCLE DAN
◉

I looked at your picture this morning.
There you are, standing in the backyard
of the little white house
on Porte Cima Pass,
your setter, May, looking up at you with adoration,
hunting days over for the two of you.

Lucky for me
you and Aunt Althy
had no grandchildren,
so when Mother and Daddy wanted a night
   on the town
I got my overnight with you.

I remember
oatmeal with raisins for breakfast
as you boil water in a little enamel pan
to sterilize the needle full of insulin
chuckling as you tease and ask
"don't you want a shot, too?"

I think of suppers of meatloaf and succotash
ending in chocolate pudding
followed by games
of Bingo and Parcheesi
which I always seemed to win.

FAMILY PORTRAITS

Granny was never a beauty.
Small and plain,
her one vanity
a crown of auburn hair.
Someone poured iodine into the shampoo bottle
and left it in the medicine cabinet.

Grandfather, tall and handsome,
hid the shame of a drunkard father
beneath the dignity
of his clerical robes.
Cruel illness transformed him
into a stumbling, shambling wreck.

Mother who knew her own beauty
loved the circus.
claimed Emmet Kelly had eyes only for her
as he gazed into the crowd under the big top.
A surgeon's scalpel
made her a gargoyle.

LILLIAN HELLMAN,
EAT YOUR HEART OUT
⊙

Mother chose the perfect hat
for her appearance
in front of the HUAC*

a snappy straw boater
trimmed in black
with just a wisp of a veil.

I can see her now,
amid the chaos
of pounding gavels and popping flashbulbs.

Demure and brave in black crepe
the hat adding just the right note
of insouciance.

What a pity
the committee
never summoned her.

* *House Un-American Activities Committee*

A Hard Act to Follow (Marriage)
❖

Daddy was married five times
but before you rush to judgment
explanations are in order.

His first "marriage"
occurred at age 18
when he, valedictorian of his class,
was approached by a pretty classmate
who claimed she was pregnant.
And, although he knew
he couldn't possibly be the father,
he "did the right thing."

When Daddyfather got wind of it,
two weeks later,
he insisted upon a divorce.
The marriage was never consummated.
There never was a baby.
Daddy went off to the state U that fall
where he fell in love
with mother's picture in a photographer's window.

Their marriage lasted 22 years
until she became ill,
dying on Valentine's Day
after suffering a torturous year.

Daddy was left spiritually and financially bankrupt
falling prey to Crazy Irene
on a business trip to Chicago.
They wed six months later

Less than a year went by
when he was forced to flee
in the dead of night
after waking to find
her standing over him
a knife in her hand.
After the divorce his lawyer told him
he was "one lucky son of a bitch."

I introduced him to Joan,
a charming divorcee,
who took one look
and pursued him across the country.
They were wed, off and on,
for the next 40 years.
He divorced her once
but she threatened suicide.
Making her wife number four and five.

Backseat Driver

I guess

Daddy

just had to be married,

which may explain why

he wed Crazy Irene

while Mother's cremains

were still cooling

in the cardboard sarcophagus

he carried in the trunk of his car

for the next forty years.

Shared Custody
◉

My daughter calls me

the drama queen

but she will never know

my greatest performance

was to stand and smile and wave

as she turned for one last look

before boarding the plane

that would take her from me

for two whole months.

LOSS

I wake at two a.m.
fretting about
the safety of a daughter
oceans away

And suddenly remember
my grandparents
outlived
two of their three daughters.

Audrey, age 18,
dying in agony
two weeks before
her big sister's wedding.

Margaret, the bride,
was to follow her
25 years later
ravaged by cancer.

As I lie in the dark,
I wonder
how parents
endure such a loss.

GENERATIONS

GRANDCHILDREN
◉

I'm afraid I've become
that classic bore,
a doting grandmother

Jacob
stealing second base
to help his team clinch the championship

Quinn
radiant in a scarlet tutu
when she receives her scholarship

Ellie
lithe as a gazelle
as she reaches for the high bar.

Blake
just turned one
a new star on our horizon.

Forgive me if I boast
but
can you blame me?

Reflections

Rosy from her bath
Ellie looks up at me and says
"I don't want to be old."

"You mean
you want to be like you are now
forever?"

"No, I want to be like Mommy,
I don't want to be old
like you."

A shadow crosses my heart
as I remember mother, dead at 45,
saying "I can never see myself as being old."

Blake, Age Two
◉

I offer dresses of pink or blue

to wear to Sissie's pre-school graduation.

She chooses pink

and, after her gold sandals are fastened,

I urge her to the mirror

where she, enchanted by her reflection,

gives herself

a resounding kiss.

Pre-School Graduation

Smartly dressed in black and white,

mortar board firmly in place,

Ellie strides up to the platform

takes a seat in the back row

where she sings every note,

each gesture down pat.

When I tell her of my pride

she appears not to hear

but the touch of her hand

on my wrist

speaks volumes.

A WISH FOR CINDERELLA
◉

The tiny princess,

swathed in pink tulle,

ensconced on a sea of green,

holds a pumpkin

we hope

will become a carriage

taking her to a ball

where midnight never chimes.

Two Hands
◉

Newborn Jacob
places his
plump pink starfish
atop my
blue-veined shell.
My heart is his.

Sex Ed 101

Where is yours?
My three year-old grandson asks
As I use the toilet
While he brushes his teeth.
My what?
Your penis.
I don't have a penis
I'm a girl.
What do you have?
I have a vagina.
You don't have a penis?
No, I don't.
What does a vagina do?
It's where babies come out.
A baby can't come out of my penis.
No, it can't.
Can I have
Some chocolate milk
In my sippy cup?

TO ELIZABETH GRACE
◉

Your dear mother
flew into the world
a gilded butterfly.

While you
blossomed slowly
into perfect pink peach.

Quinn Age Six (And A Half)

She doesn't like to lose

at games or cards

pretends to drop the dice

if the numbers don't suit

and when I ask

do you have a queen?

she glances at her hand

smiles slyly and says

GO FISH!

"I'm Glad"

Quinn reads the story about the duckling aloud and then we chat.

"Do you know anyone who is ugly?" I ask.

"No-ooo," she replies.

"If you knew someone who was ugly you wouldn't be mean to them, would you?"

"No-ooo...after all, you're old and wrinkled and I still love you."

"But does that mean I'm ugly?"

"Noooooo!"

WORDS

Blake is having issues

with pronouns.

She says me for I

him for he

them for they.

But when she says

"Me love you Grandmoth"

all is forgiven.

Juliana Harris has contributed poems to *The New York Times*, *The Mid-America Poetry Review*, *The Best Times*, *Chicken Soup for the Soul* and *The Kansas City Star*, among other publications. A native of Kansas City, Missouri, she now lives in Guilford, CT where she is a member of the Guilford Poets Guild.

www.ingramcontent.com/pod-product-compliance
Lightning Source LLC
Chambersburg PA
CBHW062106290426
44110CB00022B/2727